WOW! ME

By LOU

WOW! ME

Copyright © 2022 by LOU
Author & Original Drawings LOU
Final Illustrations I Cenzial

All rights reserved. No part of this publication may be reproduced, distributed, or transmitted in any form or by any means, including photocopying, recording, or other electronic or mechanical methods, without the prior written permission of the author, except in the case of brief quotations embodied in critical reviews and certain other non-commercial uses permitted by copyright law.

Tellwell Talent
www.tellwell.ca

ISBN
978-0-2288-6803-3 (Hardcover)
978-0-2288-6802-6 (Paperback)
978-0-2288-6804-0 (eBook)

"LOVE TO SHARE THIS WITH YOU"

About the Story

This is a story about a wonderful adventure, on the way discovering what seems to be the bestest kept secret of all time—yes, of all time!

I would love for this little book to touch and inspire the hearts of children all over the world.

"There is no other place in the Universe that we know of yet where there are Humans"

Hi
Can I share with you something I feel
seems to be the bestest kept secret of all time
yes of all time
I'm soooo excited
well here it is
are you ready
here it is
WOW!

All the love I need in my life
is inside of Me
it's there just waiting
WOW!

All I do is turn my attention
inside and feel it
WOW!

It's very quiet
so I let myself be quiet
and
WOW!

It feel's so peaceful
I can even feel my breath
WOW!

My breath
in out in out
slower and slower
softer and softer
quieter and quieter
WOW!

I love to remember this
every day
first thing when I wake up
I'm Alive
WOW!

My breath
in out in out
slower and slower
softer and softer
quieter and quieter
all the love is there
inside of Me
WOW!

Feeling this every day
I get to experience
the beauty of this life
WOW!

What a wonderful world
this is
even when things don't go so well
I can still feel the love inside of Me
how good is that
WOW!

I know life can be up and down
for all of us at times
but having this feeling of love
inside of Me
is a precious gift
WOW!

This love that's within all of us
needs to be felt
it's not a thought or an idea
it truly is a feeling
WOW!

It's soooo great that on this path
of life
whatever path that is for each of us
this gift of love
is there inside of Me
All the time
All the time
WOW!

I know I do have a choice every day
and I know I am what I practice
so I choose to feel this love
within Me
how great is that
WOW!

My breath
in out in out
slower and slower
softer and softer
quieter and quieter
there it is
such a peaceful feeling
WOW!

I'm soooo grateful that
all the love I need
in my life
is inside of Me
it's there just waiting
WOW!

This was so kindly shared with Me
now I'm sharing it with You
So when you know this for yourself
you might like to share it too
Once this little lamp of love is lit
then it can light another unlit lamp
in someone else and someone else
and someone else
WOW!
WOW!
WOW!

Oh one last thing
you need to know this love
inside of you for yourself
not just believe me

So
if this makes sense to you
how great
and if it doesn't maybe
it will sometime later

Bye

"The Earth was small,
light blue and so touchingly alone,
our home that must be protected"
Aleksei Leonov
Cosmonaut who made the 1st Spacewalk

"We are very lucky to be here"
Mike Massimino
Nasa Astronaut

"I put up my thumb and
shut one eye and my
thumb blotted out
Planet Earth,
I felt very small"
Neil Armstrong
1st Man to walk on the Moon

"I hope I go to heaven when I die,
I suddenly realised that I went to
heaven when I was born"
Jim Irwin
Drove the Moon Buggy

"Looking back on Earth,
seeing this tiny little blue ball,
you could hold it in the palm of
your hands"
Astronaut

1st Moon Landing

About the Author

My most precious book as a child was a gift from my Auntie Nonie, who sent it to me from across the seas when I was five years old. It was so exciting, coming all the way across the seas to this little person who lived in a small country town.

WOW!

I treasure this book. And now, maybe I can send my little book across the seas to you . . . WOW!

For more information,
please go to wowmebook.com.

Acknowledgments

"Love to my Mum, Dad, Graham, Prem, and all my Family and Friends and YOU"

Humans Becoming Human Again WOW!

CPSIA information can be obtained
at www.ICGtesting.com
Printed in the USA
LVHW071103230322
714166LV00011B/403